►◄ Contents

Tying Techniques for Ties

Tying Techniques for Bow Ties

Tying Techniques for Scarves and Cravats

The Tie ►◄ A Stylish Accessory for Men

The renewed delight in the tie continues! The man of today takes pleasure in wearing the only originally masculine accessory—frequently with pride—and certainly with color, design, and a knot tied to perfection. Long gone is the typical subdued gray tie that sought to be unobtrusive, but remained an obligatory bother that more likely than not was the well-meaning but annoying gift from family or family-in-law.

Times have changed in favor of the stylish tie. Contemporary colors of bright red to leaf-green, "daring" designs with, perhaps, dancing couples in the style of Art Deco, mice eating cheese, or romantic sunsets, as well as exqui-site materials such as silk, helped bring on an unanticipated renaissance for the tie. The tie is worn with style, dignity, self-consciousness, and a certain nonchalant elegance—provided, of course, that the tie or bow tie is tied in perfect form. The wearer must choose a knot which goes with the width and material of the tie while at the same time complementing the collar shape of the shirt. Only then, the tie achieves the desired effect as the accessory detail that creates the impression of the "man as work of art." This book wants to help you realize just this effect.

►◄

4

How to Tie
TIES

Michael Adam

Sterling Publishing Co., Inc.
New York

Acknowledgements

For the supply of ties, bow ties, scarves, and other objects:

Ambiance GmbH Ties and Accessories, Krefeld: 22/23, 26/27, 29 right (tie)

Halbritter, Fuchsstadt, with the brands: Sepp Halbritter, Gino Pilati,
      Sir Henry: 1 middle, 3 middle and below, 12-18, 24/25, 29 left, 38/39, 42/43

Bad Hersfeld: 1 (tie clasp), 29 right (4th and 5th clasp from the left)

Offermann, Bergisch-Gladbach (Bensberg): 37 top

Pro Idee, Aachen: 10/11

Schlips & Co., F.R. Sobiechowski Accessories GmbH, Hamburg: 40

Stange-Schleifen, Berlin: 1 right, 3 top, 30, 32, 35, 48

Translation by Annette Englander

Library of Congress Cataloging-in-Publication Data Available

10 9 8 7 6 5 4 3 2 1

Published 2004 by Sterling Publishing Co., Inc.

387 Park Avenue South, New York, NY 10016

Originally published by Falken-Verlag GmbH, Niedernhausen under the title
      Krawatten: Fliegen und Tucher perfekt binden

©1994/1995 by Falken-Verlag GmbH

English translation ©1996 by Sterling Publishing Co., Inc.

Distributed in Canada by Sterling Publishing

c/o Canadian Manda Group, One Atlantic Avenue, Suite 105

Toronto, Ontario, Canada M6K 3E7

Distributed in Great Britain by Chrysalis Books

64 Brewery Road, London N7 9NT, England

Distributed in Australia by Capricorn Link (Australia) Pty. Ltd.

P.O. Box 704, Windsor, NSW 2756, Australia

Sterling 1-4027-1512-9

Scarf ►◄ Cravat ►◄ Tie

A Brief History

In 1827 the tie, that fashionable strip of silk, wool, or cashmere, was praised by none other than the French author Honoré de Balzac (1799–1850), when he wrote, "A man is worth as much as his tie—that is, through it he displays his character, in it he manifests his spirit." At that time, the tie had already celebrated at least its 170th birthday.

The original form of the long necktie that is common today dates to the first half of the 17th century, when in Central Europe the Thirty Years' War (1618–1648) raged. Croatian mercenary soldiers wore scarves or neckerchieves whose ends were slung in a rosette and decorated with tassels which draped on the chest. The French in the reign of Louis XIV (1638–1715) named these scarves *cravate*, a corruption of "Croat."

The soldiers of the royal Croatian regiment were outfitted in a manner reminiscent of the Roman legionaries in the first century A.D. The Trajan column, built in the year 113 in Rome, shows that a scarf similar to the necktie was already fashionable in the classical world. The sculptors of the 100ft (30m) marble column honored the warriors of the cohorts of Marcus Ulipius Traianus (53–117, Roman Emperor from 98). The scarves, carved in detail, are shown tied in front of the neck and are known in

Tie wearer from the 3rd century B.C.: Terra-cotta soldier from the "army" of the Chinese Emperor Shih Huang Ti.

first Chinese emperor, Shih Huang Ti (the end of the third century B.C.). The soldiers are modeled so precisely that even the drapery of the scarves wound around their necks is clearly visible. The history of neckwear, with the moment of this discovery, extended several centuries earlier than was previously known.

▶◀

A most noble neck decoration worn with a suit of armor: The tie-fan of Louis XIV.

the history of fashion as "focales."

Until 1974, this graphic portrayal was the oldest evidence for the origin of the tie. However, in a sensational discovery, Chinese peasants attempting to dig a well near the old capital Xi'an, after the first few feet, came upon some terra-cotta soldiers. Eventually, an army of about 7500 of these terra-cotta soldiers were unearthed on the periphery of the monumental grave site of the

As far as the West is concerned, however, it is the introduction of the Croatian neckerchief to Western Europe, and especially France, that bears relevance to the origin of the ubiquitous necktie. In France, Louis XIV, the Sun King, liked everything that was beautiful. At his Court the cravat, made of linen or muslin with broad edges of lace, emerged and became fashionable. The most precious materials,

Gigantic scarves worn up to and over the chin shown in "The Meeting of the Incroyables" (around 1800).

Butterfly bow worn on the bare neck by the Marquise de Pompadour, who knew very well of the coquettish effect of her accessory.

exquisite laces, and the most expensive brocade were just good enough to be used for a cravat. His Majesty, the king, employed his own "Cravatier," whose sole job was to take care of the valuable neck decoration.

The Duchess Louise de La Vallière (1644–1710), one of the official mistresses of the Sun King, not only took a liking to Louis, but also to his cravat, which she tied, for her own decoration, into a butterfly bow. Thus was born the "lavallière," which has remained in fashion to this day in many variations.

►◄

The history of the tie advanced through an odd happenstance in the battle of 1692 of the War of Succession of the Palatine at Steinkirk (in present-day Belgium). In the early dawn of August third, an English regiment attacked the troops of Louis XIV. They completely surprised the still sleepy French officers, who had no time to

7

tie their uniform scarves according to the current style. In a rush they slung the scarves around their necks with a loose knot, letting an end hang down over the knot.

Although the French troops warded off the English surprise attack to win the battle, the English succeeded in creating the fashion "à la Steinkirk." To the name "cravat," applied

Embodiment of the dandy: "Beau" Brummel is said to have pampered himself up to six hours daily.

both in England and France, was added a variant, loosely tied with long flowing ends, called the "Steinkirk." The new style freed future wearers from the cumbersome Baroque cravat.

►◄

A hundred years later, a cutting-edge event, in the true sense, did away with many antiquated customs. It was the French Revolution: Among perhaps more momentous happenings, the "Steinkirk" and "Lavallière" fell out of fashion. The scarf was now wound in several layers up to and over the chin, as if the neck could not be protected enough.

In France these scarves, mostly of starched muslin artistically draped, were called "Incroyables." In Paris, around 1800, private lessons were given on how to tie these accessories.

In England, where the gigantic scarves became known as "napkin fashion," the legendary George Bryan Brummel (1778–1840), the original dandy, was one of its most ardent followers. Sometime after his death the style of the fold-over collar began a relentless spread. The English aristocracy adopted the long tie to make the four-in-hand acceptable. The term derived from the four-in-hand carriage that stood in waiting and could only be driven by a gentleman wearing a necktie. A related, but competing fashion was the ascot, derived from Ascot Heath, the famous racetrack near Windsor. The ascot, also called the plastron, was slung once or twice around the neck, tied in front, and often fastened with a brooch-like pin.

In France a style of narrow ties developed at yacht and sailing clubs. The narrow style became known as *régate*, preserving a hint of its origin in the elegant milieu of maritime sports. The long tie has prevailed, at least since the 1920s, to become a symbol of men of all classes caught in a fashion that seemed to have them "by the neck," with no relief in sight. But, just in time men have realized the marvelous fashion accessory that they have at their fingertips. Rather than a dreary obligatory sameness, a colorful, expressive rejuvenation has exploded, allowing men to fall in love with the personal, stylish necktie all over again.

▶◀

Even prospective kings wore modern ties: Albert Edward, son of Queen Victoria (photo from 1876).

9

►◄ Windsor ►◄

There are several varia-
tions of the classic Windsor knot. The hallmark of
the Windsor is its beautiful
symmetry, which derives
from the double wrapping
of the wide tie-end around
the neck loop.

1
*Cross the wide
end over the
narrow one to
the left (as
seen facing the
wearer) and
bring it from
behind to the
front, up and
through the
neck loop, . . .*

2
*. . . pull the
wide end
down and
wrap it behind
to the right.*

3
*Now wrap the
wide end up,
in front, and
over the neck
loop, where the
knot is form-
ing, so that the
back side shows
and extends to
the left.*

4
*Loop the wide
end horizon-
tally and to
the right, in
front of the
knot which is
being created.*

5
*Next, bring
the wide end
from behind,
up through the
neck loop
and . . .*

6
*. . . tuck it
through the
front loop that
was just
formed.*

11

Half
►◄ Windsor

This is the most compact among the slightly asymmetrical knots. The half Windsor is best tied with medium-weight ties that do not have to be as long as for the Windsor. The knot is a chic alternative to the Windsor!

1
Place the wide end to the left in front of the narrow one, . . .

2
. . . then wrap it behind and upwards through the neck loop.

3
Bring the wide end over the neck loop to the left, then to the right behind where the knot is forming, so that the back side shows.

4
Now wrap the wide end again to the left over the narrow end where the knot is forming, . . .

5
. . . and bring it once more behind and upwards through the neck loop. Then, . . .

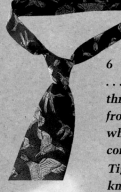

6
... *tuck it through the front loop, which has come about. Tighten the knot and slip it into shape at the collar.*

Simple ►◄ Knot

This is the knot for beginners—it's easy to learn and remember. This knot is equally suitable for ties made of silk or wool. At the collar, this knot looks somewhat asymmetrical.

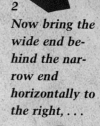

2
Now bring the wide end behind the narrow end horizontally to the right, . . .

1
Cross the ends of the tie so that the wide end lies over the narrow end and points to the left.

3
. . . then wrap it in front of the narrow end, where the knot is forming . . .

4
. . . and pull it behind and upwards through the neck loop.

6
Finally, tighten the knot, carefully press it into shape, and nestle it against the collar.

5
Now all that needs to be done is to tuck the wide end down through the front loop, which was just created.

Double Knot

3
Now comes the double-wrapping; the wide end is wrapped again behind the narrow one, pointing to the right . . .

This knot gets its compact form through double-wrapping. It is especially suited to narrower, somewhat longer ties that are unlined and of light fabric.

1
Cross the ends so that the wide end goes over the narrow one and points to the left.

2
Wrap the wide end once around the narrow one all the way so that it crosses in front again and points horizontally to the left.

4
. . . and brought back over the front so that it points again to the left.

5
Bring the wide end behind and up through the neck loop . . .

6
. . . and then tuck it down through the front loop of the double-wrapping. Carefully align the knot, and shape it so that the double-wrapping becomes visible.

►◄ Shelby

This modern knot, also known simply as the "American" knot, is best suited for shorter ties with a heavy lining. In form and look, it resembles the Windsor.

4
Now fold the wide end horizontally from left to right over the narrow one, . . .

1
Cross the ends with the back seams facing out; the narrow end lies above the wide one and points to the right.

5
. . . and bring it again up through the neck loop.

2
Bring the wide end forward, up, and over the neck loop. Pull it down with the back seam still showing.

3
Draw this wrapping tight.

6
Finally, tuck the wide end down through the just-created front loop, draw the knot tight, and align it.

Freestyle

◄►

The name tells it all: This knot freely combines elements from the tieing of other forms, specifically the Windsor and the simple knot. If you use a medium-weight silk tie, the knot will not be too bulky.

1
Cross the ends so that the wide end runs to the left on top of the narrow one.

2
Wrap the wide end behind the narrow one horizontally to the right, and fold it up in front of and then through the neck loop to the left, so that the back seam shows.

3
Now wrap the wide end horizontally back to the right, . . .

4
. . . and bring it again up through the neck loop.

5
. . . Tuck it down through the just-created front loop.

6
Finally, draw the knot tight and shape it at the collar.

◄► New Classic ◄►

This is a "dainty" knot, distinguished by its especially slender vertex at its base. It succeeds best with medium-weight ties that are not long.

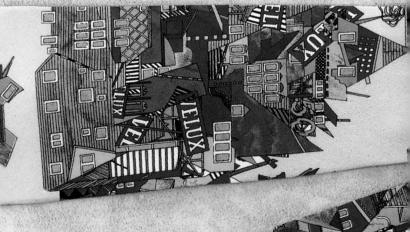

2
Bring the wide end up so that the smooth side faces out, . . .

1
Cross the ends with the back seams facing out; the narrow end lies above the wide one and points to the right.

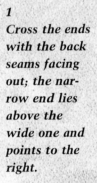

3
. . . then pull it through the neck loop horizontally to the right, . . .

6
Draw the knot tight, and shape it at the collar.

4
. . . and wrap it back over the narrow end horizontally to the left.

5
Now bring the wide end from behind up through the neck loop and tuck it through the just-created front loop.

►◄ Cross Knot ►◄

1
Cross the ends with the smooth side facing out. The wide end lies above the narrow one at first, pointing to the left; then it is

This knot, which was "presumed dead" for quite some time, was very popular around the turn of the twentieth century. The idea for including this stylish binding comes from the Swedish tie-maker Amanda Christensen.

wrapped behind the narrow end so that it points to the right with the seam facing out.

2
Fold the wide end up and through the neck loop so that it points to the left with the seam facing out.

3
Now wrap the wide end completely around the narrow

one so that it again points to the left, . . .

4
. . . fold it once more to the right, and pull it up through the neck loop.

6
Draw the knot tight, making sure that the double wrapping remains visible.

5
Bring the wide end down through the just-created double-wrap front loop.

Diagonal ►◄ Knot

One of the most unconventional—and most difficult—ways to tie a tie is the eye-catching diagonal knot. The knot, invented by David Mosconi, is especially effective with subdued patterns.

1
Cross the ends so that the wide end lies above the narrow one and points to the left, with the smooth sides facing out.

2
Now wrap the wide end beneath the narrow one so that it points to the right with the seam facing out, . . .

3
. . . and wrap it once completely around the narrow end so that it again points to the right.

4
Next, bring the wide end from the front up through the neck loop so that it points to the left with the seam facing out, . . .

5
. . . and then tuck it down through the just-created front loop.

6
Draw the knot tight by twisting it slightly as you shape it and push it upward.

27

Pins ►◄ Tacks & Co. ►◄

Filigree and valuable: Tiepins dating from the period 1850 to 1920.

The ring is made more beautiful by the stone; the pendant ennobles the necklace; nicely made buckles decorate the belt. The dress of people in everyday life, especially of women, is enlivened, enhanced, and brought to perfection by the accessory of jewelry.

►◄

And the tie? It is the principal accessory that men have to dress themselves up. We might think that that is enough. Yes, it may be, but the necktie also has its own special accessory: the tiepin.

The origins of these delicate accessories trace back at least to the second half of the 18th century.

The pins were needed to fasten the cumbersomely tied silk or lace ties in front of the chest. These tiepins naturally became a focus of decoration. About 130 years ago, it was then the plastron or ascot that caused the gentlemen of society to stream to the jewelers.

With the falling out of fashion of the plastron and success of the stylish long tie, the tiepin was no longer the practical necessity it began as. The tie tack, widely called by the earlier name "tiepin," replaced the long stick-style pin. Whether as tack or pin with a little chain, whether made of fine gold or gold plate, the tie tack holds the ends of the tie in place at the shirt. None-

28

theless, its predominant role is as decoration to enhance the tie and add a further individual touch.

Some other tie accessories have emerged, but

their widespread use is yet to be established. There is, first of all, the collar clasp, which draws the two collar wings close to the knot while pressing the knot slightly upward. In some settings, this clasp can be quite attractive when worn without a tie! This is not the case with the tie stick, a second related accessory. It can be used only with a

shirt that has the respective holes in the collar. The tie stick also supports

the knot from below, which should be taken into consideration when selecting a style of knot. Another accessory that should be mentioned is the tie ring. It is used for ties and foulards, which, slung twice around the neck, are

Whether elegant or humorous, tie tacks have become increasingly popular since the 1950s.

pulled through the tie ring. All these accessories for the tie give men opportunities for personal and expressive creativity in their appearance. It might be considered, however, that it is only in the harmony of jacket, tie, collar, knot, and pin that the nature of the man presents itself!

29

►◄ Men Choose Their Ties Themselves ►◄

Will a tie go with a polo shirt? Never. Should you tuck your tie into the trousers' waistband? Faux pas! How about a narrow, gray leather tie? Totally dated!

Smart bow tie for the highly official occasion! Better not!

Unfortunately, there are, after all, plenty of ways to embarrass oneself with a tie, a bow tie, or a scarf. It is no wonder, therefore, that men may tend to be conservative and occasionally insecure when trying to figure out what is suit-able for which occasion in which combination. Some basic rules:

- The man of the world combines the tuxedo and the related white dinner jacket with the bow tie, which is usually unobtrusive in color, but on occasion may be colorful with patterns. Also with tails, a bow tie is worn—of course made of white piqué. The cutaway, which has become rare, is decorated by the plastron or ascot with a pearl.

- For other occasions the rule is simply to use your intuition and discerning eye to select exactly the right tie for the event—one that balances your outfit and sets the appropriate mood.

It was Marlene Dietrich, the famous film star, who claimed that a woman alone was capable of glancing at another woman and in the same instant meticulously evaluating everything about her, while maintaining an air of casual indifference. The same could be said of men, today. One man assesses the other with exactly the same dissecting sharpness at first sight, while appearing to make no judgments at all. The viewer instantly picks up clues from the other's dress, manner, and,

The appropriation of male fashion: Marlene Dietrich in jacket and tie (photo from 1931).

especially, choice of tie and its presentation to speculate on what he does for a living, how much money he makes, what his marital status is, how sophisticated he is, whether he lets someone else choose his wardrobe, and so on.

Men can exhibit their taste by selecting each tie, bow tie, or scarf themselves. The scarf, in particular, has more and more been appropriated as a decorative accessory by women. Women also frequently wear tied bows of one sort or another. But, it is different with the necktie: fashion has several times tried to adopt the long necktie for women—without overwhelming success. Curiously, the long necktie remains a male symbol and a man's most definitive accessory.

A close association can be established between a person and his dress: The bow tie has been a favorite for the political campaigner.

31

Traditional ►◄ Bow Tie

This bow tie style is only distinguished very slightly from the classical bow tie style presented on pages 34 and 35. The principal distinction is that the traditional form is more suitable for bow ties that

3
Next, bring the right end all the way down behind the neck loop, . . .

are cut with a wider "waist," since it is not tied as tightly.

1
The left end of the bow band is folded back on itself and then placed in a central position to form an overall loop.

4.
. . . and tuck the dangling end through the just-created front loop, pulling from right to left.

2
From below, the right end is wrapped straight up with the narrow piece of the band crossing the middle of the folded left end.

5
Finally, draw the bow tie tight, and tug it into shape.

Classical Bow Tie ►◄

For the classical bow tie, the middle loop is gathered up a little more tightly than for the traditional style. Therefore, this variation is especially suitable for bow ties that are cut with an extremely narrow "waist."

1
Cross the bow bands with the longer end lying on top.

2
Pull the longer end behind and up through the neck loop so that it points to the left.

3
Now fold the shorter end back on itself, giving the "bow" shape.

4
Bring down the upper end so that it hangs straight down with the narrow band crossing the middle of the folded end.

5
Fold the dangling end also back on itself in the "bow" shape, and bring this folded end around the other bow, tucking it behind this first bow through the middle loop.

6
Finally, bring the bow tie into the right form by tugging it—perfect!

►◄ Ties Need to Be Handled ►◄ with Care!

*How to Keep Your
Neckties Looking New*

There are those, believe it or not, who simply loosen their good necktie, slip the loop over their head with the knot still tied, and hang it in the closet or on the back of a chair until the next time

A smart solution for wrinkles: the tie press.

they need to put it on. The unfortunate tie is left to wrinkle with no thought about its proper care. Well, there are times when we may be forgiven for such treatment, such as the

quick visit to the health club between appointments or the unexpected

►◄

denouement of a night out where the hastily removed tie lies, knot still tied, in a pile on the floor. The question then is: How do you deal with the wrinkles and get your tie looking fresh again?

Typically, men have resorted to using an iron with lots of steam. This usually works, but more than one tie has been irreparably scorched. Nowadays there is a better solution: a tie press. The

36

Practical solutions for travel and at home: (Top) shirt and tie bag; (Above) swivel tie rack for the closet.

press is suited for any tie, whether made of silk or polyester, linen or cotton. The tie comes out perfectly smooth in only 20 or 30 minutes. Generally, the heavier the silk, the less danger of wrinkles. A tie that is always untied and properly stored should keep its original form indefinitely.

⋈

Whereas wrinkles can be removed relatively easily and expertly, stains are a big problem, not so neatly solved. The truth is hard to admit, but a tie that has been stained with fat, red wine, lipstick, or similar substances is ruined. Experience has shown time and again that dry cleaning robs the tie of its brilliance. A dry-cleaned tie is likely to find its place in the secondhand thrift shop beside ties that fashion left behind. After all, as with women's dresses it can be said that nothing is as old as last year's tie!

⋈

Neckslip ►►

The "neckslip" is the modern variation that connects
the long necktie with its
origins. It is worn with the
neck loop beneath the
shirt collar. It is a fashionable, extravagant acces-
sory!

1
*Place the neck-
slip around
the neck in
such a way
that the wide
end lies to the
right (as seen
facing the
wearer).*

2
*Now bring the
wide end
through the
loop sewn at
the end of the
narrow
piece . . .*

4
*Finally, fold
the wide end
forward and
tug it into
whatever form
you prefer.*

3
*. . . and pull it
up through the
neck loop.*

►◄ Plastron ►◄

The plastron or ascot had
its heyday in the 19th century. Today this almost
forgotten type of tie is
worn only for official occasions—say, as an elegant
accessory for the cutaway.

1
*Place the neck
scarf loosely
around the
neck and cross
it in such a
way that the
upper end
points to the
left (as seen
facing the
wearer).*

2
*Pull the left
end up
through the
neck loop, . . .*

3
*. . . and then
bring it down
to the left . . .*

4
*. . . and fold it
under itself,
but on top of
the other end,
horizontally,
to the right.*

5
*Bring the long
right end
through the
just-created
loop, and
draw both
ends tight.*

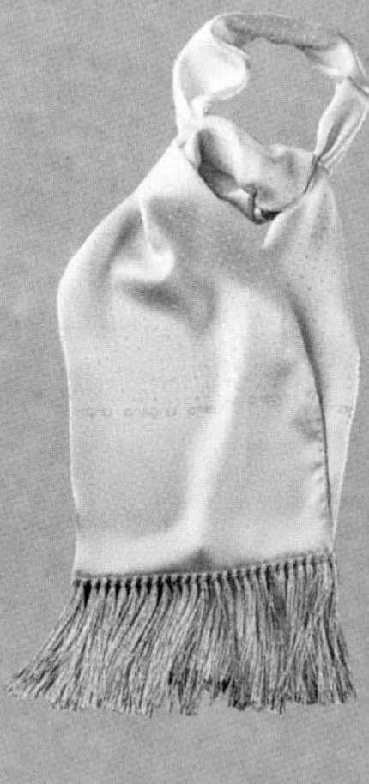

6
Finally, tug the knot into shape. The ends of the scarf can be crossed in front of the chest and fastened with a tiepin.

Rendezvous ►◄

Whether aristocratic lady-killer or bon vivant: This scarf knot certainly exudes sensuality.

1
Cross the scarf ends with the end on top pointing to the right (as seen facing the wearer). Wrap the right end behind, up, and over the neck loop.

2
Wrap the right end again behind, up, over the neck loop and, then, tuck it behind and through (left to right) the double front loop just created.

3
Draw the knot to the desired degree of tightness, and finish by tieing off the ends with a simple square knot (right over left; left over right).

4
The knot is enhanced by folding in the ends.

Limited Edition Works ▶◀ of Art ▶◀

Ties from the Designer's Workshop

Ties made of handsawn alabaster applied to plywood! A long tie made of recycled cardboard with airbrush motifs! Bow ties made out of window screen plated with platinum—today, anything is possible.

Designer fashion has made its presence felt in neckwear. These are unique ties—at most, very limited editions—which were made by hand and, of course, were certificated. In other words, designer ties belong in the category "artworks." And thus, for most people, they are excluded from being an accessory. The strictly limited editions of art ties are generally quickly out of circulation and are too valuable to really be used for day-to-day wear.

▶◀

Dangers lurk everywhere. Thus, just as attempts are made on famous paintings, ties too—in any case, valuable designer ties—are never quite safe from the desires of others to possess them. Even intentional destruction of a favored or valuable tie is not unheard of. A few years ago a man unwittingly found himself in the middle of a local festival in a region of Europe where, on a certain

A lacquered wood tie that is flexible (and thus wearable) by virtue of attached leather strips.

44

day, women are given license to cut off the tie of any man, according to some old custom. The incident resulted in the unfortunate man filing a lawsuit. The case specified the destruction of his limited-edition silk tie, one of only 250, embroidered with a number and the artist's monogram. The court decided, as others before, that destruction of property is still destruction of property whether committed as part of a festival or not.

Really, designer ties are not meant to be thought of or used in the same way as more ordinary ties. But even the best, most fashionable ties meant to be worn have a short life as one fashion season gives way to the next. It is considered that faithfully holding on to old ties in the belief that you will one day wear them is a definite mistake.

Designer tie made of silk (Lagerfeld Collection).

For the gentleman with extravagant taste: a tie with appliqués of reflective materials.

45

On the Tie ►◄
Style ►◄
►◄ and Fashion

A Journey of Quotations Through the Centuries

Oscar Wilde

A man is worth as much as his tie—that is, through it he displays his character, in it he manifests his spirit.

Honoré de Balzac (1799–1850), French writer

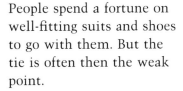

People spend a fortune on well-fitting suits and shoes to go with them. But the tie is often then the weak point.

Maurizio Marinella (born 1956), Italian tie designer

►◄

A beautiful and unusual tie is simply a conversation piece: It triggers conversations—in a restaurant, at a meeting, on the road.

Frank Rudolf Sobiechowski (born 1956), German tie expert

A tie, today, must have something to say.

André Stutz (born 1948), Swiss tie and fabric designer

►◄

Fashion is what one himself wears. Old-fashioned is what the others wear.

Oscar Wilde (1856–1900), Irish writer

►◄

Real elegance means to stay within earshot of fashion.

Marie Baroness of Ebner-Eschenbach (1830–1916), Austrian poet

►◄

Fashion is a charming tyranny of short duration.

Marcel Achard (1899–1974), French dramatist

A man does not have to wear a tie in order to look elegant. It is nothing more than a decorative detail.

Giorgio Armani (born 1934), Italian couturier

▶◀

Style is the human being himself.

Georges Louis Leclerc, Comte de Buffon, (1707–1788), French naturalist

▶◀

Style is the dress of thoughts.

Philip Dormer Stanhope, Earl of Chesterfield (1694–1773), English statesman

▶◀

Wolfgang Joop

Style is very simple: To decide on the correct Yes or No.

Wolfgang Joop (born 1944), German couturier

▶◀

The art of the tieing of ties is for the man of world what the art of giving dinners is for the statesman.

Emile Marc Hilaire (1793–1887), French writer, alias Marco de Saint-Hilaire

▶◀

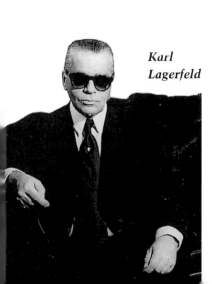

Karl Lagerfeld

I love ties—but only wear black ones. I never leave my house without a tiepin. I love wide ties. Without a tie I feel dingy.

Karl Lagerfeld (born 1938), German couturier

Index ►◄